A Li...

Vijaya Kumar

NEW DAWN PRESS, INC.
Chicago • Slough • New Delhi

NEW DAWN PRESS GROUP

Published by New Dawn Press Group
New Dawn Press, Inc., 244 South Randall Rd # 90, Elgin, IL 60123

New Dawn Press, 2 Tintern Close, Slough, Berkshire, SL1-2TB, UK

New Dawn Press (An Imprint of Sterling Publishers (P) Ltd.)
A-59, Okhla Industrial Area, Phase-II, New Delhi-110020

A Little Book of I Ching
Copyright © 2004, New Dawn Press
ISBN 1 932705 13 9

All rights are reserved. No part of this publication may be reproduced, stored in a retrieval system or transmitted, in any form or by any means, mechanical, photocopying, recording or otherwise, without prior written permission of the original publisher.

NOTE FROM THE PUBLISHER

The author specifically disclaims any liability, loss or risk whatsoever, which is incurred or likely to be incurred, as a consequence of any direct or indirect use of information given in this book. The contents of this work are a personal interpretation of the subject by the author.

PRINTED IN INDIA

Contents

Introduction 5

How I Ching Works 6

The Hexagrams 12

Preface

This books is by no means an extensive study by any professional. The data provided in this book are my own interpretations of the subject, gleaned from various books, and presented from a layperson's viewpoint.

The book deals with each aspect of the study, point by point, in a simple language, and serves as a ready reckoner for those who have no time to go through heavy, in-depth studies.

The publisher and I hold no responsibility for any discrepancy in the script. We would welcome suggestions or intimation of errors that come to anybody's notice.

Vijaya Kumar

Introduction

Timeless wisdom is enshrined in the ancient Chinese book, I Ching, or Book of Changes. I Ching is an accurate system of predicting the future, which is based today on casting of coins, drawing hexagrams and interpreting them.

Of all the divinaing methods, the I Ching is considered to be the purest form. It states that change is a constant, enduring force pervading everything and everywhere.

The highest aim of the I Ching, like all ontological systems is self-knowledge. This books reveals all that you want to know about marriage, children, business, health, travel, fortunes, etc.

How I Ching Works

1. The universe is made up of five elements, and according to the Chinese system of divination, they are water, fire, wood, metal and earth.
2. All things, animate and inanimate, are made up of these elements in varying proportions.
3. These proportions and element change during evolution in a constant manner with the passage of time.
4. If the rate of change of these elements can be asscertained, then the future course of events can be pinpointed to time and place.
5. Based on these principles, the Chinese evolved a system that symbolised 64 life situations, represented by lines, solid and broken, in 64 different forms of line arrangements, called the hexagram (similar to the Indian Pancheekarana).
6. I Ching is similar to the Binary system for by substituting a zero for each broken line and a one for each solid line of a hexagram, one can get the Binary scale from zero to 63.
7. I Ching has 64 hexagrams consisting of six broken or solid lines, texts and commentaries.
8. The basic symbolic unit of the hexagram is a trigram which consists of three lines, broken or solid, or a combination of both.

   ___ ___   _____
   broken line   solid line

9. By various combinations of broken and solid lines, you can get a maximum of eight trigrams.

10. By combining these trigrams in different formations, you get 64 hexagrams.
11. These lines, trigrams and hexagrams are symbolic of the forces of action and change that occur in the universe.
12. The broken lines represent the yin force that is female, docile, negative, weak and passive, as also being destructive.
13. The solid lines represent the yang force that is male, virile, positive, strong, active and constructive.
14. Yin and yang forces are constantly interacting, creating change that is constant.
15. While the yin is dark, receptive, weak, yielding and representing the earth, the yang is light, creative, strong, firm and representing the heaven.
16. Three coins are cast six times. Each throw gives one line, and six throws give six lines, thus forming a hexagram. (Note: One can use a 5-paise, 25-paise, or the old 20-paise coin for casting.)
17. For each throw, you get either Heads or Tails. Assign 3 for Heads and 2 for Tails (i.e., give 3 for the side which has no value, and 2 for the one with value).
18. The trigrams with their attributes, images and family relationships are shown on the next page.
19. The following values can emerge:
    2 + 2 + 2 = 6 = Moving Yin (old)
    Symbolised by —— —— x
    2 + 2 + 3 = 7 Yang (young)
    Symbolised by _____
    2 + 3 + 3 = 8 Yin (young)
    Symbolised by —— ——
    3 + 3 + 3 = 9 = Moving Yang (old)

	Trigram	Name of trigram	Meaning	Attribute	Symbol	Family Relationship
1.	☰	Ch'ien	The creative	Strong	Heaven	Father
2.	☷	K'un	The receptive	Devoted, yielding	Earth	Mother
3.	☳	Chen	The arousing	Excited, Moving	Thunder	Eldest son
4.	☵	K'an	The abysmal	Dangerous, Cunning	Water	Middle son
5.	☶	Ken	The quiet	Stubborn, keeping still	Mountain	Youngest son
6.	☴	Sun	The yielding	Gentle, penetrating	Wind, Wood	Eldest daughter
7.	☲	Li	The clinging	Agitated, beautiful	Fire, Sun Lightning	Middle daughter
8.	☱	Tui	The joyous	Soft, laughing	Lake	Youngest daughter

Symbolised by _____ x

Draw a broken line for a yin, and a solid line for a yang. All the coins adding to the value of six depict the first line (all 3 coins were tails) which represents the moving yin line, marked by an x. The line with the value of nine (all 3 coins fell as heads) represents the moving yang line, marked by an x.

20. The moving yin and yang, considered to be laden with extreme inner tension, alter their polarity and assume their opposite roles and traits.
21. All hexagrams are built up from the bottom line to the top, since all organic life grows upwards.
22. The moving yin and yang lines are called old lines which change to their opposites at any one or several points in the six lines.
23. The moving yin line (6 or _ _ x) represents the future, relating to the meanings given for any particular line, while the moving yang line (9 or _____ x) represents the past or the present.
24. A moving yin changes into a yang, known as progression, while a moving yang, changing into yin is called retrogression.
25. In each hexagram, the lower two lines indicate earth, the middle two man, and the last two heaven.
26. A yin or broken line spells misfortune, while a solid line or yang indicates good fortune and as being constructive.
27. Too many yin lines, or yang lines, in a hexagram shows imbalance.
28. Once the hexagram is drawn, read the judgement and the image, plus the commentary on the line, which will give the general conditions of the hexagram.

29. Any moving line, indicated by an x against it, should be given importance, for it transforms into future state of affairs and forms the resultant hexagram, which will be the final assessment.

e.g.

Casting coins six times -

Result – 6, 7, 8, 8, 7, 8 =

$6 = 2 + 2 + 2 =$ — — ⟶ Moving yin
$7 = 2 + 2 + 3 =$ ——   Trigram
$8 = 2 + 3 + 3 =$ — —   K'an

$8 = 2 + 3 + 3 =$ — —
$7 = 2 + 2 + 3 =$ ——   Trigram
$8 = 2 + 3 + 3 =$ — —   K'an

By referring to the hexagram chart, we find that the hexagram is 29.

Read all about the judgement, image and the commentary on the line, then turn to the new hexagram produced by the first Line which is moving line, and the new hexagram will be 59.

Old hexagram   New hexagram

$6 = --x$ ⎤   — ⎤
$7 = ——$ ⎬ K'an   — ⎬ Sun
$8 = --$ ⎦   — — ⎦

$8 = --$ ⎤   — — ⎤
$7 = --$ ⎬ K'an   — ⎬ K'an
$8 = --$ ⎦   — — ⎦

Hexagram 29   Hexagram 59

Hexagram Chart

Trigrams Upper → Lower ↓	Ch'ien ☰	Chen ☳	K'an ☵	Ken ☶	K'un ☷	Sun ☴	Li ☲	Tui ☱
Ch'ien ☰	1	34	5	26	11	9	14	43
Chen ☳	25	51	3	27	24	42	21	17
K'an ☵	6	40	29	4	7	59	64	47
Ken ☶	33	62	39	52	15	53	56	31
K'un ☷	12	16	8	23	2	20	35	45
Sun ☴	44	32	48	18	46	57	50	28
Li ☲	13	55	63	22	36	37	30	49
Tui ☱	10	54	60	41	19	61	38	58

The Hexagrams

1. CH'IEN - The Creative

- The upper and lower trigrams are both Ch'ien.
- All lines are solid and represent yang—male, active, strong, giving, mentally and spiritually-oriented and consistent.
- Ch'ien, with the attributes of heaven, the king, the leader and the family head, represents a person using his power constructively.
- Since primal energy becomes its opposite on reaching its climax, this hexagram warns of failure if strength is excessive.
- **The Judgement**: Ch'ien means a force of success flowing from the depths, and as such man strengthens himself by this active force, keeping his energy in store.
- **The Image**: This means that heaven moves unceasingly, making the self strong, effective and enduring.
- **The Lines**

  Nine in the bottom line: The dragon symbolises dynamic force, but at present is lying dormant. So wait patiently for your moves.

  Nine in the second place: Your situation will improve and your efforts will be appreciated. Try to get advice from your elders.

  Nine in the third place: Much has to be done which will fetch no great dividends. Avoid pitfalls and maintain balance in difficult times.

Nine in the fourth place: You will have to decide whether to strike upwards or withdraw. There is no question of 'right' or 'wrong' way; the guiding force is within yourself.

Nine in the fifth place: Your talent may be recognised by an influential person who will help you. You will influence others and meet other influential people, but you will also be in a lonely position.

Nine in the sixth place: You will be bound to be isolated materially and mentally if you continue in this way (arrogantly).

- **Fortune**: Fairly good.
- **Marriage**: The man will be a good husband while the woman may be a dominating wife.
- **Children**: More boys than girls, and they should be well-disciplined to avoid their being arrogant.
- **Health**: Chest and head complaints, but recovery is possible if condition is serious.
- **Employment/Business**: No change in job. Routine business will be successful.
- **Finance**: You will feel the pinch at most times. Gambling will be disappointing.

2. K'UN: The Receptive

- Each line represents earth, the dark, mother force, yin, showing devotion and shouldering responsibilities.
- Like Ch'ien, this is a primary force.
- The first two lines represent the king and the queen, or the father and the mother.
- These lines indicate that being receptive you can be constructive when led by the Creative or Ch'ien.

- **The Judgement**: You should be guided and supported. With peaceful perseverance, you will achieve good fortune.
- **The Image**: It is in the nature of the earth to sustain everything, good or bad. Since the man is pure and deep in character, he can accept and support his situation.
- **The Lines**

    Six at the bottom: There are signs of impending misfortune.

    Six in the second place: The Receptive yields to the yang force, resulting in things turning out well.

    Six in the third place: Your quiet efforts will bear fruits later.

    Six in the fourth place: Act with extreme caution in case things go wrong, and be reserved.

    Six in the fifth place: This will be the time of achievements, but indirectly and discreetly, especially in public.

    Six at the top: Beware of danger, law suits and quarrels, where both sides may be hurt.
- **Fortune**: Good
- **Marriage**: An obedient, meek, devoted wife.
- **Children**: More girls than boys who will all be happy.
- **Health**: Infection of the abdominal region. Though not serious, negligence could lead to a critical condition.
- **Employment/Business**: Wait for a better opportunity.
- **Finance**: Money will flow in steadily but unexpected expenses my leave you in a fix.

3. CHUN–Difficulty in the Beginning

- The above trigram is K'an and the one below is Chen.
- Both these two trigrams bring clouds, rains, and thunder together.

- This will be a time of tension.
- You will have to wait patiently for the tense period to be over, before venturing into anything.
- **The Judgement**: Be warned of premature and precipitate action which will bring disaster, but great perseverance will bring success.
- **The Image**: You should wait for the difficult period to be over and take advantage of better conditions after the rains.
- **The Lines**

    Nine at the bottom: Be decisive, but avoid hurrying and forcing the pace. Simply be diligent and humble.

    Six in the second place: Shock and sudden change of affairs. Adopt a high-powered approach and avoid help from anyone which will lead to obligation. Only when this cycle of troubles is over will success follow.

    Six in the third place: Deep disgrce is possible by a premature action when there is lack of guidance. A person in trouble may hold you back. Avoid forcing issues.

    Six in the fourth place: An unusual chance should be grabbed. Recognition follows after some embarrassment.

    Nine in the fifth place: Maintain your rhythm step-by-step, always being correct and not in expectation of success.

    Six at the top: Arrogance and a sudden twist in events can result in great ill-luck. A right attitude is required.
- **Fortune**: Bad.
- **Marriage**: Unhappy unless late marriage.
- **Children**: Many, but first birth very difficult.
- **Health**: Ear, nose, heart and kidneys may be affected and become serious, but there will be a gradual cure. Neurosis is also likely.

- **Employment/Business**: No chance for the present. Wait for a better opportunity.
- **Finance**: Problems arise, but help may be sought from women and inferiors.

4. MENG–Youth

- This hexagram denotes immaturity and purity.
- The upper trigram is Ken which stands for the youngest child or mountain, while the lower, K'an, means danger or water.
- Here, youth, the foolish one, requires instruction.
- The youth has to be patient and consistently forbearing.
- **The Judgement**: The foolish child needs to be tutored, and he has to learn to accept the relationship of master and pupil. He will, on advice, learn to be respectful and hardworking.
- **The Image**: One should refine one's character with clarity and perseverance.
- **The Lines**

    Six at the bottom: The youth must have a serious approach if he has to get over being foolish and unappreciative. Meaningless, constricting routines may stunt the mind. A time of difficulty, which may ease out.

    Nine in the second place: A time of harmony and achievement. This line shows the person to be strong of mind, assisting the weak, and gearing up for higher responsibility.

Six in the third place: To safeguard your dignity, remain modest, quiet and correct.

Six in the fourth place: Cease all associations with an unrealistic person who will only bring humiliation.

Six in the fifth place: It is very necessary to avoid any preconceptions, and to have respect for one's teacher. Success is assured.

Nine at the top: Caution is required, for you may be punished or you may be the punisher, but be fair with the punishment.

- **Fortune**: Bad.
- **Marriage**: Failure in love, and not a good match in marriage.
- **Children**: Their future will be good.
- **Health**: Contagious disease affecting the heart and abdomen. Recovery will be very slow.
- **Employment/Business**: Slow in coming.
- **Finance**: Trouble with paying bills–insufficient funds.

5. HSU–Contemplation (Nourishment)

- Indications of rain-clouds in the sky suggest that one must bide one's time.
- Contemplation here suggests that the vital energy is in the centre of the body and you will have to wait to activate it at the proper time.
- You need to be cautious as well as ambitious.
- Be warned of competition, but do not treat the competitors harshly.

- **The Judgement:** You will recognise situations for what they are with an inner certainty. You must be resolute, and consistent in your action and application. Travelling making major decisions, or great changes is favourable.
- **The Image:** Waiting and preparing for the future will be fruitful.
- **The Lines**

    Nine at the bottom: Feeling agitated and dissatisfied. Be careful to lead a well ordered and planned life.

    Nine in the second place: Remain calm and generous during times of strife, and things will resolve favourably.

    Nine in the third place: Be careful in relationships, and safeguard your possessions and status.

    Six in the fourth place: Since you are isolated and in a dangerous situation, be composed and patient. Chances of success are remote, and you can only try to survive.

    Nine in the fifth place: By maintaining a calm and relaxed attitude, enjoy your good fortune. Proceed slowly towards your goal.

    Six at the top: Disaster will strike, and it is wise to give in gracefully. A ray of hope should motivate you to be cautious and alert which will benefit you.
- **Fortune:** Fairly good.
- **Marriage:** In love, wait with expectation for good results. Delay in marriage is sure.
- **Children:** Late childbirth.
- **Employment/Business:** Wait for good opportunities.
- **Health:** Rest and nourishment will cure all digestive ailments.
- **Finance:** Unexpected money will be receivedafter waiting for some time.

6. SUNG–Conflict

- The upward movement of heaven (Ch'ien trigram) is in conflict with the downward flow of water (K'an trigram), suggesting conflict.
- Complications arise out of work or project half completed.
- This hexagram also suggests a quarrelsome nature, so guard against all disputes.
- Foreign tour should be avoided.
- **The Judgement**: Instead of being egoistic and stubborn, try to be clear-headed and fair enough to compromise. Seek advice from a wise person. Avoid undertaking any venture which requires concerted energies.
- **The Image**: Conflict can be prevented only by careful and meticulous planning of aims.
- **The Lines**

  Six at the bottom: Avoid confrontations and forcing things which may lead to disputes on which eventually will clear up if they do take place.

  Nine in the second place: Avoid confronting anyone bigger than yourself. Quiet living will do you good, otherwise it will lead to a conflict.

  Six in the third place: No successes or failures, so do not seek praise or acclaim. Depend upon what you have earned or discovered.

  Nine in the fourth place: A conflict will show you in the wrong, and by turning back, peace will prevail. A recent loss will be followed by fortune.

Nine in the fifth place: Someone higher up will give you wise counsel. You will gain recognition or promotion when deserved.

Nine at the top: Conflict follows after seeming success over others, giving unhappiness. Nothing gets settled. Quiet living will find life easy.

- **Fortune**: Bad.
- **Marriage**: Failure in love and marriage.
- **Children**: A son who will be having conflict with his father.
- **Health**: Many complications affecting the brain, lungs, kidneys and the blood system.
- **Employment/Business**: Unable to find a job. If able, those in job will face demotion or punishment. Business will be dull.
- **Finance**: Disappointing. An old lady or an inferior will help you tide over things.

7. SHIH–The Army

- The unbroken line in the lower trigram denotes a leader. As it is in the lower trigram, it denote only head of an army not the head of a state.
- As a person of authority he has control over the powerful forces of the army, and so must act correctly and trustfully.
- For the army to remain effective, he must have the respect of his men.
- There will be many hurdles and hardships which can be overcome only by strict discipline.

- **The Judgement**: Since the situation warrants a strong man, the person must command respect by demonstrating the common needs and his fitness to lead.
- **The Image**: Only one who follows peacetime policies will have support in war. Similarly, there should be trust and common values between those undertaking a venture together.
- **The Lines**

    Six at the bottom: Good time to start new ventures or to forge ahead, but be sure that they have good motives and principles, otherwise serious trouble is in store.

    Nine in the second place: An influential person will help your progress. Promotion and recognition are assured, and your success will be shared by your associates.

    Six in the third place: Misfortune follows due to your overestimation of your virtues and overlooking your weaknesses. Whatever apparent success follows will be without value.

    Six in the fifth place: You need to be more vigorous and experienced to be an effective leader.

    Six at the top: Even when obstacles are overcome, and situations improve, be careful of your complacency and unfair methods.
- **Fortune**: Bad.
- **Marriage**: Will not have a good match, and problems will arise.
- **Children**: More daughters than sons.
- **Employment/Business**: Marginal gain, and strong recommendations may fetch success in employment.
- **Health**: Heart and abdominal diseases, malignant tumours, chances of accidents.
- **Finance**: Will come and go.

8. PI–Union

- This indicates a person or time of cooperation and goodwill.
- If there is honesty, trust and commitment, then good fortune in personal and business dealings is definite to follow.
- This also indicates peace after war or quarrels.
- You will mix with others and get close to them, thus harmonising relationships.
- **The Judgement**: Since new entries in a group cannot share the same depth of union as the earlier members, it would be wise to accept everything of the union as it stands, else leave the group.
- **The Image**: Just as water is absorbed by the earth, forming a natural union, so did kings award lands to their nobles for them to understand the assets of union.
- **The Lines**

  Six at the bottom: You should be sincere and appreciative for true relationships to endure. You may get help in work.

  Six in the second place: Respond freely to others which will endow you with dignity. Formal relationships may not be smooth. Unusual help may be expected.

  Six in the third place: Beware of others' attitudes and avoid intimate relationships with unsuitable characters that will weaken you.

  Six in the fourth place: Stick to your principles. You are closely in contact with someone at the centre of a union, so do not hide your relationship.

Nine in the fifth place: Do not force anyone into a union. There will be difficulties at first but will ease out but by correct conduct.

Six at the top: A time of difficulty. Do not vacillate but either commit yourself or withdraw.

- **Fortune**: Good.
- **Marriage**: A very good match with happiness and harmony.
- **Children**: Children will bring happiness and be loyal to you.
- **Health**: Long lifespan beset with curable ailments resulting from impure blood.
- **Employment/Business**: Joint undertakings are favourable. Greed will bring loss. New business brings success.
- **Finance**: Good.

9. HSIAO CH'U – The Restraining

- This denotes that a strong person will be obstructed by niggling constrictions, forcing him to compromise.
- Any venture that he begins will be impeded by the same constrictions.
- Though the time is not conducive to business, step-by-step progress will improve it.
- Female predominance is indicated.
- **The Judgement**: Though success is indicated, it can come only through subtle and friendly methods, if one does not give in to temptation.
- **The Image**: As the forces of circumstance prevent achievements of lasting significance, you should express

yourself openly in small ways to those around you, and take time to develop your skills.

- **The Lines**

  Nine at the bottom: Instead of forcing issues, bide your time and act in harmony with the nature of time which will bring fortunes.

  Nine at the second place: You can achieve your objectives if you do not push forward but join the others in the direction they take. Promotion may occur.

  Nine in the third place: By attempting to surge forward, you invite trouble, and friends will be unsympathetic, seeing you as overbearing and crude.

  Six in the fourth place: You wield some influence by being close to the centre of events. You must recognise harsh truths and then take appropriate action. You can amend things if you are sensitive and honest.

  Nine in the fifth place: Selfless cooperation with others will lead to success. Promotion and recognition are in the offing.

  Nine at the top: Do not attempt harsh measures, but have an impassive attitude and wait.

- **Fortune**: Fairly bad.
- **Marriage**: Not successful as ill-matched.
- **Children**: Children will give you anxious moments and they need to be disciplined.
- **Health**: Possibility of, venereal disease, diseases of the uterus, chest and abdomen, if care is not taken.
- **Employment/Business**: Setback in both.
- **Finance**: You may make a little money.

10. LU–Treading

- This hexagram suggests that you should be genteel, and act in accordance with the established norms.
- You also need to observe great caution in dangerous circumstances.
- The weaker ones will unusually be able to prevail upon the strong.
- Be humble and patient to avoid any unforeseen dangers.
- **The Judgement**: As a loner, you will be forced into contact with presumably inferior beings, but danger lurks. So act with dignity, and remain sensitive.
- **The Image**: Your attitude towards others should be appreciative, otherwise you can become unrealistic and biased.
- **The Lines**

    Nine at the bottom: You can progress with conscientiousness and good work, but you are in danger of losing the simple virtue which could give you good fortune.

    Nine in the second place: You will pursue inner goals, understand fate and move contentedly.

    Six in the third place: You are in danger of exposing yourself to various conflicts and losses.

    Nine in the fourth place: Danger and trouble stalk you, but with the courage of your convictions you will be able to move ahead.

    Nine in the fifth place: Difficult times ahead, but be constantly aware of danger and avoid recklessness.

Nine at the top: If your past has been good, your future too will be so.
- **Fortune**: Fairly good.
- **Marriage**: Fairly good.
- **Children**: They will pose problems earlier, but will be good later on.
- **Health**: Generally good, though mild infection of the lungs and brain are indicated.
- **Employment/Business**: Hardships and hurdles.
- **Finance**: A slight loss.

11. T'AI–Peace

- This hexagram suggests a strong force creating harmony with the weaker force by being pliant and conceding.
- It generally indicates harmonious conditions.
- The male will be refined with a soft and gentle approach, though characteristically strong, while the female will be blessed with beauty.
- Your fortunes will multiply.
- **The Judgement**: Deep harmony in relationships and circumstances prevail due to your strong, creative traits.
- **The Image**: Pay attention to the inner truths which in harrmony with nature.
- **The Lines**

    Nine at the bottom: As a man with influence and a constructive approach, work with like-minded people towards common goals. Gains are likely.

    Nine in the second place: Remain pleasant and correct by not being snobbish or dismissive towards lesser mortals, when you find life flowing smoothly.

Nine in the third place: If everything seems normal, be cautious and correct to prevent them becoming bad, and if things are bad, remain calm.

Six in the fourth place: Don't attempt anything new which could be a disaster. Be open and sincere with all.

Six in the fifth place: Try to adjust with your inferiors which can bring happiness. Promotion, recognition and union are on the cards.

Six at the top: Trouble of all kinds will brew, but they can be eased out by a humble and generous attitude.

- **Fortune**: Good.
- **Marriage**: A happy one.
- **Children**: They will have good fortunes, but their education needs attention.
- **Health**: Good, with slight head ailments.
- **Employment/Business**: Success with good planning.
- **Finance**: Good, but you need to be watchful.

12. P'I–Disharmony

- The hexagram indicates poverty, decay and acrimony.
- There is no chance of any constructive result.
- Indications are of a person who is arrogant, strong and loud, but inwardly weak.
- There is disharmony in life.
- **The Judgement**: In all the confusions, there is no gain in action; so concentrate on maintaining affairs humbly and with dignity.
- **The Image**: Do not get involved in anything for an easy gain, social or financial. By being pure even in hardships, your nature gets refined and good fortune ensues.

- **The Lines**
  Nine at the bottom: Be wary in choosing companions. Steer clear of anything worthless or of disrepute, and avoid new ventures.
  Six in the second place: Be quiet and humble in your dealings, and avoid inferiors, or defensive attitudes.
  Six in the third place: Be careful of not being involved in slander or humiliation. Those ashamed of their conduct will not change their ways.
  Nine in the fourth place: As the disharmony lessens, adopt a bold, principled approach to avoid further harm. You may gain from others.
  Nine in the fifth place: Using your strength and virtue, restore order amidst confusion.
  Nine at the top: Beset with loss, sorrow and difficulties, you will yet manage to get through them with proper efforts.
- **Fortune**: extremely bad.
- **Marriage**: Ill - matched, may lead to breakup.
- **Children**: Disharmony amongst the children.
- **Health**: Respiratory and brain disorders likely. Cancer is indicated.
- **Employment/ Business**: Dull time for profits.
- **Finance**: Difficult period likely.

13. T'UNG JEN–Social Fellowship

- The top trigram Ch'ien signifies heaven, while Li, the one below, denotes fire, both of which are in harmony.
- A brightly shining sun in the heaven indicates benefit to farmers and communities in general.

- The broken line in between suggests a gentle influence in the midst of male dominance.
- The broken line is also suggestive of wisdom and concern for all which bind men together.
- **The Judgement**: Social cooperation and friendship with shared goals and common activities promotes great progress under the leadership of an orderly person.
- **The Image**: It would be wise to stay within the limits of universal principles.
- **The Lines**

  Nine at the bottom: Be honest and open, and cooperate with others who will reciprocate if the principles are grasped.

  Six in the second place: Avoid exclusive contacts, snobbishness, quarrelling factions, pettiness and shallow discrimination. Some bitterness and restrictions are likely.

  Nine in the third place: Be humble. Your over-individualistic nature can alienate you from others, and your mistrust of them can make you obnoxious in their eyes.

  Nine in the fourth place: Your foolish mistakes will be exposed by difficulties and you may be defensive.

  Nine in the fifth place: Difficult conditions will improve. Adjustments will ease a wearisome association. Lovers may be parted.

  Nine at the top: An alliance which lacks warmth is indicated. The indication of remoteness shows no real satisfaction to be gained from one's state of affairs.
- **Fortune**: Good.
- **Marriage**: Women will be happy, but not men.
- **Children**: Many children who will live in harmony.
- **Health**: Good.

- **Employment/Business**: Good profit, partnership will be beneficial, good employment prospects, opening of branches likely.
- **Finance**: Enough money.

14. TA YU–Possession in Abundance

- Fire (the upper trigram Li) in heaven (the lower trigram Ch'ien) indicates glory and riches.
- The broken line of Li is indicative of success which has been achieved through humility.
- Spiritual more than materialistic living is indicated.
- Caution is also necessary, for there is fear of falling down.
- **The Judgement**: This is the time for regulated strength and fruition. This also indicates that the weak owns the strong by his unselfish virtue.
- **The Image**: Be cautious when you are rich in happiness or wealth, otherwise this will result to complacency and an evil bent of mind.
- **The Lines**

    Nine at the bottom: Be sensitive and maintain your principles to face forthcoming difficulties. Harm is indicated, as also accrual of wealth.

    Nine in the second place: For some this signifies burden, causing movement restriction, while for others it shows mobility. Goals can be achieved with the help of others.

    Nine in the third place: While great people utilise their wealth for the good of others, petty people use it for selfish ends. Energetic rather than retiring people benefit now.

Nine in the fourth place: Be unmoved or unaffected by other people's wealth.

Six in the fifth place: Be restrained for there is a possibility of trouble with others.

Nine at the top: Even when you are successful, be modest and virtuous, and do make a pilgrimage to offer thanks in praise of God.

- **Fortune**: Extremely good.
- **Marriage**: You will have a rich suitor and a happy marriage.
- **Children**: Will be skilled and promising.
- **Health**: The lungs will be afflicted but recovery will be rapid.
- **Employment/Business**: Prestigious position in job. Good business.
- **Finance**: Great income and great expenditure.

15. CH'IEN–Modesty

- You will be very modest which will be apparent.
- You possess spiritual qualities and are practical.
- This hexagram also suggests a simple, unglamorous quality elevated in spirit.
- You will win the confidence and trust of your friends.
- **The Judgement**: Even with wealth and position you will be polite and modest that will lead to success.
- **The Image**: The wise man understands that his fate is destined, and thus, by adjustments and avoidance of extremes, leads a harmonious life.

- **The Lines**
  Six at the bottom: Being modest of your capabilities, you can achieve great undertakings. New responsibilities and success will accrue.
  Six in the second place: By maintaining your true modesty, you will discover new opportunities.
  Nine in the third place: Be modest and work in a quiet way to achieve success, and then guard against immodesty.
  Six in the fourth place: Do not use your position as an excuse for weakness, but remain modest. Act now for significant advances.
  Six in the fifth place: Conflict is likely, though your virtue (modesty) is recognised. Even if the necessary steps may be severe, take action if the situation requires it. Seek help from others if need be.
  Six at the top: Conflicts and difficulties can be overcome by putting things right at home, and a careful self-examination. Guard against squandering away your virtues which fetched you success.
- **Fortune**: Fairly good.
- **Marriage**: Happy.
- **Children**: Gentle, loyal and obedient.
- **Health**: Diseases related to the abdomen likely. Low blood pressure. Non-indulgence will ensure a long lifespan.
- **Employment/Business**: Not good for new business. Proceed slowly in everything.
- **Finance**: Moderate.

16. YU–Enthusiasm

- You will possess enormous enthusiasm and creativity.
- Be cautious while applying energy without care or preparation.
- Be warned against using forceful methods.
- Never lose self-control even during times of heady success.
- **The Judgement**: It is a good time to start new ventures, and seek support of others and adjust to their needs.
- **The Image**: The powerful forces of time can be balanced and steadied only through a correct interaction between spiritual and material considerations.
- **The Lines**
  Six at the bottom: Benefit accrues only if you are modest in manner and lifestyle.
  Six in the second place: Great improvement is possible if you are sensitive and pay close attention to the signs of the times, retreating and advancing as necessary.
  Six in the third place: Anticipate rapid progress or decline, and act accordingly.
  Nine in the fourth place: You can inspire others by your influence and confidence. One succeeds, and others share the benefit.
  Six in the fifth place: You feel weighed down by problems, unable to act effectively or express yourself openly due to feeling restricted.
  Six at the top: Do not be swept away by overenthusiasm, as this will give you a rude awakening.
- **Fortune**: Fairly good.
- **Marriage**: Smooth.

- **Children**: Great future for them as they live in harmony.
- **Health**: Liver and abdominal problems indicated, but will recover.
- **Employment/Business**: Both are good and indicative of profits.
- **Finance**: Expenditure more than income.

17. SUI–Following

- This hexagram indicates that an older man defers to a young girl.
- The person will be happy and pleasant.
- He is full of creative power.
- Willingness to follow will fetch good fortune.
- **The Judgement**: To become a powerful leader, you should yield to certain demands, however unnecessary or foolish they may be. Persevere to establish harmony and confidence amongst your supporters.
- **The Image**: A time for easy gain or loss, more so the latter. Conserve your efforts and adapt to situations.
- **The Lines**
  Nine at the Bottom: Do whatever is right, even though, as a leader, you will have to adapt to your friend's needs.
  Six in the second place: You may have to choose between remaining (and so miss an opportunity), and leaving.
  Six in the third place: Stick to your aim, and gain will follow if your conduct is good.
  Nine in the fourth place: Be careful of your ego when you are successful through your influence. Good fortune is likely through your influence. Good fortune is likely through others.

Nine in the fifth place: You are correct and constant with a rock-firm ambition. Promotion and success are on the cards.

Six at the top: This indicates that you would rather retire from your position.

- **Fortune**: Fairly good.
- **Marriage**: Successful though delayed.
- **Children**: Harmony with parents.
- **Health**: A prolonged period of sickness from which recovery is possible. Kidney failure is likely.
- **Employment/Business**: Chances not bright. Wait for better times.
- **Finance**: Good income and likewise expenditure.

18. KU–Reparation of the Spoiled

- This hexagram signifies ruin and destruction.
- But indications of change are also present.
- Hard work will be necessary.
- Incompatible arrangements are indicated in settled businesses, communities or relationships.
- **The Judgement**: Imminent loss and trouble are indicated, and this is the time for repairing the damage done. Always consider and contemplate before and after beginning.
- **The Image**: When ruin looks imminent, hard work and orderly reorganisation will establish solid conditions.
- **The Lines**

  Six at the bottom: The rot has set in but it can be stemmed by careful planning and hard work.

  Nine in the second place: This situation has resulted due to weaknesses, and you need to change your outlook.

Nine in the third place: Error and criticisms result due to overenthusiastic corrections of past mistakes.

S : in the fourth place: Things are deteriorating due to your negligence, but yet they can be amended if care is taken.

Six in the fifth place: Amendment and corrective measures bring cheer from colleagues. A time for new undertakings perhaps.

Nine at the top: Do not relax, but concentrate on higher aspirations.

- **Fortune**: Bad.
- **Marriage**: Ill-matched.
- **Children**: They will create problems, and you need to correct them instantly.
- **Health**: Have a complete check-up, for you may have abdominal problems.
- **Employment/Business**: No scope for anything new.
- **Finance**: More expenditure than income.

19. LIN–Conduct

- **Fi**
- This indicates kindly authority and good relationship between two people.
- Joy and forbearance are indicated.
- This is a time of good fortune.
- Indications of further good fortune are there.
- **The Judgement**: A time of good fortune, growth and energy, but guard your conduct and be aware of the signs of the times.

- **The Image**: Indications are of a supercilious manner due to one's elevated position. So educate by setting a correct example to those inferior to you.
- **The Lines**
  Nine at the bottom: A time of improvement, promotion and success. Seek help from elders if possible.
  Nine in the second place: A fortunate time for one who is cheerful, has the determination to succeed, and understands the laws of life.
  Six in the third place: A time of worry and sadness. Try not to be careless and offensive once in a comfortable position.
  Six in the fourth place: Indications are of success, harmony and favour from superiors for working people.
  Six in the fifth place: A time of smooth achievement for a leader who is wise in delegating work to the right people.
  Six at the top: Success or harmony is indicated, and one will return to pass on the benefit of his experience.
- **Fortune**: Extremely good.
- **Marriage**: Good.
- **Children**: Loyal, obedient and well-mannered.
- **Health**: Diseases related to the stomach.
- **Employment/Business**: Good with profits.
- **Finance**: Savings will be depleted.

20. KUAN–View

- It is a time to settle down now, and not try anything new.
- It is also a propitious time for study, and the pursuit of spiritual and religious matters.

- By honesty and kindness, you can ease out the present state of mess.
- Unexpected assistance will brighten your prospects of success.
- **The Judgement**: People in charge of projects, or wielding influence over others, must be sensitive to their responsibilities. The subject will meditate and also contemplate.
- **The Image**: Great benefit will be brought by a wise, strong and influential person, who is a symbol of clarity and balance.
- **The Lines**

  Six at the bottom: A time of unrealistic thinking, plenty of activity with little success.

  Six in the second place: It is better to be involved in humble and gentle activities now, and avoid a narrow, self-centred view. Concentration is required for a difficult work.

  Six in the third place: Caution is required now with a lot of ups and downs. Objective self-examination is indicated.

  Six in the fourth place: One with a balanced view of the past and future will enlighten you about social process, and you should honour him. You may benefit from travel or be promoted.

  Nine in the fifth place: Promotion and success are likely. To counteract your selfishness, strive to do good for others through all your actions.

  Nine at the top: A time of difficulties. Indicates a wise and strong man who transcends all personal feelings and mundane matters.
- **Fortune**: Fairly good.
- **Marriage**: Frequent quarrels.

- **Children**: Children, will cause worries; need to be disciplined, but they will shape up well.
- **Health**: Ailments related to the abdomen, need to be disciplined, and they will shape up well.
- **Employment/Business**: Not smooth at present.
- **Finance**: Not good.

21. SHIH HO–Biting Through

- This suggests a person who bites his way out through obstacles and critical situations.
- Legal action may be taken for getting out of tight situations.
- Finally, justice will be given.
- Take forcible action, but proceed cautiously.
- **The Judgement**: Balance has to be achieved in administering justice, and carefully consider everything before acting.
- **The Image**: Difficulties arise and one needs great clarity and determination to get out of them.
- **The Lines**

    Nine at the bottom: The time of loss, demotion or punishment can be overcome with caution and care.

    Six in the second place: Either you are wronged, or you will have to take the decision to amend the wrong.

    Six in the third place: An old problem will be difficult to solve, and it has to be handled correctly. Success is likely, otherwise criticisms.

Nine in the fourth place: Though this is a time of gain, avoid being excessive, for great difficulties have to be dealt with a tough hand.

Six in the fifth place: Meet your responsibilities with a positive attitude, and you will have profits.

Nine at the top: This denotes a rogue who, despite warnings, has allowed evil to gather momentum which means demotion, slander, conflicts and unpopularity, with the likelihood of his losing the job.

- **Fortune**: Bad.
- **Marriage**: Difficulty at first, but happiness later.
- **Children**: A compassionate approach towards strong-willed children will yield good results.
- **Health**: Nervous breakdown is likely.
- **Employment/Business**: Obstacles and losses.
- **Finance**: Money will come and go.

22. PI–Gracefulness

- This indicates a young couple.
- Beauty and energy are also denoted, and these should be handled with sensitivity for them to last.
- This also suggests that while the woman will age gracefully, the man will be still youthful and irresponsible, denoting impermanency or beauty being short-lived.
- The warning here is also that beauty can be only skin-deep.
- **The Judgement**: This hexagram stresses the fact that a beautiful form can be hollow within.

- **The Image**: Only trivial matters should be dealt with routinely. Gracefulness and sensitivity will help in everyday work.
- **The Lines**
  Nine at the bottom: A person with a humble beginning will advance, if he is active.
  Six in the second place: Do not become involved in petty self-consciousness or superficialities. Accept help gracefully.
  Nine in the third place: While in a complacent and mellow condition, do not neglect your responsibilities. A time of easy success.
  Nine in the fourth place: One has to make a choice between having widespread popularity and having simple, close communication with one or a few special friends, but indications are toward a simple lifestyle.
  Six in the fifth place: Empathy and sincerity being more important to you than material equality, you seek a higher way of life, and eventually, all will go well.
  Nine at the top: Form and content are in recognisable unity in a balanced condition. You should stick to simple undertakings for a successful living.
- **Fortune**: Fairly good.
- **Marriage**: Choose your partner carefully and your marriage will be good.
- **Children**: Weak and often falling ill.
- **Health**: Serious problems and needs immediate attention.
- **Employment/Business**: Moderate success and profit.
- **Finance**: Fair, not much money flowing in.

23. PO–Disintegration

- This indicates decay, dissolution and misfortune.
- The season being indicated is autumn, and everything starts to decay and disintegrate.
- The five yin lines indicate weak, dark forces ascending to overcome the strong.
- The hexagram shape is indicative of a house ready to collapse with only walls and roof remaining.
- **The Judgement**: A time of misfortune, when one's affairs are in a bad state.
- **The Image**: Face problems with equanimity and selfless behaviour. The situation can be saved from disaster with absolute firmness.
- **The Lines**

   Six at the bottom: You will have to wait patiently and face the ruinous conditions bravely.

   Six in the second place: One has to take prompt action to ward off imminent disaster, which may prove overwhelming.

   Six in the third place: Instability will still continue, and one should seek to compromise, or exit for which one will not be blamed.

   Six in the fourth place: Misfortune can no longer be avoided.

   Six in the fifth place: Gradual success and recognition are indicated.

   Nine at the top: Understand and be sensitive to all experiences, for good fortune is assured if you are correct and careful.

- **Fortune**: Extremely bad.
- **Marriage**: Not successful.
- **Children**: Either none, or if any, will be sickly.
- **Health**: Lung and heart ailments.
- **Employment/Business**: Neither will be good or profitable.
- **Finance**: Loss due to others.

24. FU–Returning

- This indicates a decrease in bad fortune.
- The solid single line represents the warm, creative yang force rising.
- The upper trigram K'un (earth) encompassing the lower trigram Chen (wood), symbolises the roots of a plant.
- This hexagram represents potential success, imminent advancement, and new, lucrative opportunities.
- **The Judgement**: Like-minded people join harmoniously together in new undertakings, suggestive of the creative forces returning after retreating.
- **The Image**: Treat everything carefully and do not hurry in any matter, following the principle of rest while the life energy is held within the earth.
- **The Lines**

  Nine at the bottom: A time of material rewards, and to return to the true path from which one has digressed a little.

  Six in the second place: Be aware of the excitement, creativity around you, and others' creative ideas, even if you have to swallow your pride.

Six in the third place: Changing condition with no great successes or failures are denoted.
Six in the fourth place: A change for the better will urge you to act that is certainly for the best, though you may be alienated from others.
Six in the fifth place: Minor losses are possible, though success is indicated finally.
Six at top: An opportunity missed will necessitate a quiet, humble and repentant attitude.

- **Fortune**: Good.
- **Marriage**: Happy and joyful.
- **Children**: Many children who will be good and will have a good education.
- **Health**: An old ailment may catch up again. Indications of stomach and bowel disorders.
- **Employment/Business**: Good for both.
- **Finance**: Good.

25. WU WANG–Simplicity

- The top trigram is Ch'ien whose attribute is creative, heavenly law.
- The trigram below is Chen which denotes movement and strength.
- This hexagram indicates a natural and happy state of affairs.
- New undertakings can be taken now.
- **The Judgement**: You will need to have purity and genuine innocence coupled with perseverance in order to achieve success.

- **The Image**: Sudden or unexpected changes in conditions are possible, though the fundamental force is creative and growing. So it is necessary to be adaptable, guileless and natural.
- **The Lines**

    Nine at the bottom: Listen to your intuition, for this is the time of harmony and god fortune.

    Six in the second place: Fulfil all your tasks, and complete them, for this is the time of advance.

    Six in the third place: Profit for some, loss for some are indicated, and disappointments for others.

    Nine in the fourth place: A time of moderate success. No chance of making a mistake if you are true to your essential characteristics.

    Nine in the fifth place: Sudden misfortune will affect you deeply, but if you retain clear simplicity within, react spontaneously and freely; things will then clear up.

    Nine at the top: Do not trust your instincts for this is not the right time for progress. Cunningness is needed for tricky situations.
- **Fortune**: Fairly good.
- **Marriage**: Sudden marriage (arranged) in which both have to be sincere and self-sacrificing towards the other in order to make the marriage work.
- **Children**: Good fortune and education are in store for the many children born.
- **Health**: Respiratory and nervous disorders are likely.
- **Employment/Business**: Good for employment. Honest business will fetch profits.
- **Finance**: Disappointing.

26. TA CH'U – Great Power in Restraint

- This hexagram indicates great potential force.
- Just as a river restrained within a dam produces energy, so are you blessed with great reserves of energy.
- You will wield a great restraint upon a creative force.
- You will have a source of spiritual and practical or material nourishment.
- **The Judgement**: Indications are of storing one's energies, conserving one's virtues by constant efforts, and some useful discipline like meditation. Physical and psychic energies in harmony show success.
- **The Image**: Indications are of storing material wealth or enduring truths, and of a person who should now be wary of becoming complacent and needs others' confidence.
- **The Lines**

  Nine at the bottom: Bide your time till difficulties wane or retreat, and be content with small improvements.

  Nine in the second place: Conserve your energies, for struggling against a superior force is futile. Advancement through another's efforts is likely.

  Nine in the third place: Keeping your aim firmly in mind, plan sensible alternatives in case your path is blocked by dangerous obstacles. Hard work will be rewarding.

  Six in the fourth place: A time of potential success, and, with foresight, one can thwart great danger or difficulties.

  Six in the fifth place: A time of good fortune and fame.

  Nine at the top: A time of promotion, recognition and success in many fields.

- **Fortune**: Fairly good.
- **Marriage**: successful.
- **Children**: They will cause problems, but later will compensate for that.
- **Health**: Chest and abdominal ailments which are curable by special treatment.
- **Employment/Business**: Both good
- **Finance**: Good.

27. I–Nourishment

- The hexagram resembles an open mouth, through which nourishment passes.
- The above trigram, Ken, is the mountain, and the one below, Chen, is wood or vegetable matter or plants and herbs which suggest good nourishment.
- The imagery of thunder rolling down the mountain (Ken) suggests nourishing rain.
- There is harmony and moderation in nourishment.
- **The Judgement**: One must be careful in discriminating, while eating, between all that is pure and beneficial, and all that is unworthy.
- **The Image**: Difficult conditions or people should be tamed, for later they will be useful.
- **The Lines**

    Nine at the bottom: Work unobtrusively, for this is the time of conflict due to criticism of one's behaviour.

    Six in the second place: Being a time of good and bad fortune, a person who is normally self-reliant or with a regular income or nourishment begins to be negligent, and hence may experience ill-effects.

Six in the third place: One's misconduct could lead to poor fortunes and decline in one's progress in life.

Six in the fourth place: Being a time of gain or loss one either seeks help in a worthy enterprise or being in a responsible position, looks for others to support him.

Six in the fifth place: Do not undertake any great ventures, and when one has no strength to help others, one should seek influential or wise help.

Nine at the top: Good fortune and success are indicated, and one who is in harmony with nourishment, will nourish others.

- **Fortune**: Fairly good.
- **Marriage**: Not very good.
- **Children**: Need to be well-reared and educated.
- **Health**: Stomach, teeth, abdomen and throat are the parts that can cause serious problems.
- **Employment/Business**: Fairly good.
- **Finance**: Good.

28. TA KUO–Excessive Greatness

- The top trigram, Tui, represents water or lake.
- The lower trigram, Sun, represents wood or tree.
- The two trigrams suggest trees under water, or flood.
- This hexagram, indicating excess, warns of a dangerous situation.

- **The Judgement**: In spite of inevitable troubles, one will be able to withstand oncoming difficulties by a gentle application of the understanding.
- **The Image**: One must have the attitude of being firm like the tree (Sun, lower trigram), and being joyous (Tui, top trigram), for all pleasant or profitable things will not last.
- **The Lines**

    Six at the bottom: By being diligent, hardworking, and cautious, you have an opportunity to advance as you choose.

    Nine in the second place: This is a time of being rejuvenated and achieving advancement, when unusual liaisons and partnerships are successful.

    Nine in the third place: This indicates the warning signs of an approaching peril, for signs of stubbornness will only lead to trouble.

    Nine in the fourth place: A complaint attitude will help smoothen daily affairs, and one can expect recognition or promotion.

    Nine in the fifth place: In this time of difficulty, it would be wise to be balanced in one's relationships.

    Six at the top: A time of sadness. Assess the situation carefully before taking steps or decisions.
- **Fortune**: Bad.
- **Marriage**: Sorrowful, with separation likely.
- **Children**: Many children, needing proper guidance and education.
- **Health**: Spinal column and lung ailments. Elephantiasis likely.
- **Employment/Business**: Not good.
- **Finance**: Poor.

29. K'AN–The Deep

- K'an, both trigrams being the same, suggests danger, crisis and involvement in conflict.
- It can denote an attitude to life, like one who constantly faces crises in order to give meaning to life.
- The dangerous situation warrants adjustments.
- One can be hurt, as well as have advancement and inner development with proper behaviour.
- **The Judgement**: With calm within, one can move quickly forward to avoid calamity.
- **The Image**: One should influence others with one's own virtue, and improve oneself constantly.
- **The Lines**

   Six at the bottom: If you lack purpose, awareness or defensiveness now you may be demoted or reprimanded.
   Nine in the second place: Small undertakings will help, though difficult conditions have to be endured.
   Six in the third place: One with a quiet lifestyle must be diligent and humble, while the active one must expect severe conflicts.
   Six in the fourth place: Be sincere even in difficult times, and everything will proceed from then on towards good contacts. It is likely that you will be sad.
   Nine in the fifth place: Too many difficulties from which one needs to escape. It is also the time to achieve goals smoothly, if conditions are favourable.
   Six at the top: Bad luck dogs one due to one's misdeeds, leading to entanglement and restraint, which fortunately, is not permanent.

- **Fortune**: Bad.
- **Marriage**: Troubled.
- **Children**: Need care and discipline.
- **Health**: Heart attack, kidney trouble or peritonitis may become serious, leading to death.
- **Employment/Business**: Wait for a better opportunity.
- **Finance**: Bad.

30. LI–Fire

- Both trigrams are Li (brightness, fire, clinging).
- This could refer to a quarrelsome, fiery, energetic person, or an assertive male lover whose loud affections camouflage his dependence on someone else.
- The fire-like energy must be restrained for it to be constructive, and not become destructive.
- It could also mean clinging, an attribute of fire, suggesting radiation of its glory.
- **The Judgement**: One should be amenable in one's behaviour in order to develop clarity and understanding, and it vital for a fiery person to acknowledge dependence on someone else.
- **The Image**: Since the sun-like attributes of Li, that is doubled, emphasises cyclic time and regularity, one should follow this quality so that its influence spreads without limit.
- **The Lines**

    Nine at the bottom: An indication of tangled disputes which requires you to be wary but pleasant.

Six in the second place: A time of harmony, success and recognition.

Nine in the third place: Trouble and dangers are indicated, and keeping your virtue, you must continue to enjoy what you have.

Nine in the fourth place: Conserve your energies, and avoid arrogance, for this line indicates consumption of oneself or the person on whom one feeds.

Six in the fifth place: Initial difficulty and great upset followed by good fortune, and development towards a peaceful, virtuous nature.

Nine at the top: An auspicious time but one may be lonely. Things should be amended rather than destroyed.

- **Fortune**: Fairly good.
- **Marriage**: Good.
- **Children**: Many and they will be blessed with good education.
- **Health**: Fever, eye and abdominal problems indicated.
- **Employment/Business**: Good
- **Finance**: Average.

31. HSIEN–Stimulation

- The lower trigram, Ken (youngest son or young man) yields to the top trigram, Tui (youngest daughter or young woman).
- This indicates that each partner yields his/ her needs to that of the other.

- This denotes persistent, quiet strength stimulating a weaker party which reacts joyously.
- This also indicates affection and sensitivity to others.
- **The Judgement**: A successful and harmonious relationship is the keynote of this hexagram.
- **The Image:** Indications are of a calm, receptive character, who, though strong, willingly subordinates himself to the needs of the weak.
- The Lines

    Six at the bottom: Be patient and observant, for your hasty, superficial approach could lead to trouble.

    Six in the second place: Wait until you have a strong principle or condition to base your action. Otherwise this is a pleasant period.

    Nine in the third place: Be cautious in your behaviour, and curb any thoughtless action.

    Nine in the fourth place: Conflict between self and others, or between narrow considerations and inner truth will leave one exhausted and ineffective.

    Nine in the fifth place: Expect conflict, and avoid being stubborn and amoral, though your firm solutions are good.

    Six at the top: Since the stimulation is only talk, nothing good or bad comes of it, and no concrete results accrue.
- **Fortune**: Extremely good.
- **Marriage**: Surely smooth-going.
- **Children**: Highly educated, and they live in harmony.
- **Health**: Chest or venereal diseases are likely.
- **Employment/Business**: Very good for both.
- **Finance**: Good income and equal expenditure.

32. HENG–Continuity

- In this hexagram, Chen (eldest son, thunder) is above the Sun (eldest daughter, gentle wind) trigram.
- This denotes that Chen is active, and leads the receptive, Sun.
- An enduring, consistent relationship is indicated.
- Honesty and sincerity are the constant companions.
- **The Judgement**: The personal qualities of strength and wisdom are in continuity, and one perseveres at every instant.
- **The Image**: The harmony of true continuity is emphasised, and through thunder and wind, the two heavenly forces, keep moving and changing. They too are subject to the laws of life.
- **The Lines**

  Six at the bottom: Be careful, sensitive and skilful in all you do for enduring results.

  Nine in the second place: One can avoid difficulties and attain a stable position by controlling excessive enthusiasm, grandiose ambitions or improbable desires.

  Nine in the third place: Avoid unnecessary conflicts which may start as minor ones and erupt into larger ones.

  Nine in the fourth place: A time of frustration and some loss, so tread carefully along the right path.

  Six in the fifth place: Be consistent, and avoid any trickery. While a woman should be conservative, a man should cling firmly to inner truth.

Six at the top: Avoid new undertakings now, and try to regain your inner composure to be in tune with your surroundings.
- **Fortune**: Fairly good.
- **Marriage**: Troubled.
- **Children**: Well-mannered and pleasing.
- **Health**: Chronic diseases likely.
- **Employment/Business**: Smooth.
- **Finance**: Fairly good.

33. TUN–Retreat

- The two trigrams are Ch'ien (older man, leader) above Ken (mountain, stillness).
- This hexagram suggests an isolated mountain hermit.
- The focus is on retreat from potentially harmful conditions.
- A person will be withdrawn and resigned, accepting conditions as they are.
- **The Judgement**: The wise person retreats, gives way, and he has to preserve so that retreat is constructive.
- **The Image**: Keeping a dignified distance between oneself and disturbing influences, one must be cautious against negative feelings.
- **The Lines**
  Six at the bottom: Since difficulties are imminent, it would be wiser to retreat quickly, if necessary, else, be calm and avoid undertaking anything new.

Six in the second place: Seek the strength or help of a superior person, and remain calm and unperturbed.

Nine in the third place: Expect complications during retreat, which could be frustrating and dangerous.

Nine in the fourth place: Withdraw gracefully to avoid any loss.

Nine in the fifth place: Retreat carefully at the right time, so that everything moves smoothly and the existing links do not get severed.

Nine at the top: This is the time of retreat, if necessary, of waiting, if planning to start enterprises, and of success in established firms.

- **Fortune**: Fairly good.
- **Marriage**: Not good or ideal.
- **Children**: Will not be loyal.
- **Health**: Chest, abdomen and bone diseases likely.
- **Employment/Business**: Not good at present.
- **Finance**: Not very good.

34. TA CHUANG–Great Power

- The top trigram is Chen (thunder), while the lower one is Ch'ien (heaven).
- The image is that of a young man endowed with vital power.
- Here, the creative forces move upwards, and depict strength and favourable outcomes.
- During favourable conditions there is great danger of misuse of power.

- **The Judgement**: While one is blessed with great power, one has to be sensitive to issues of importance to produce good, fruitful results.
- **The Image**: Thunder moving towards heaven, and both rising, show harmony which must be guarded by doing nothing nonsensical or foolish.
- **The Lines**

    Nine at the bottom: A time of peril, conflicts, regret and unpopularity.

    Nine in the second place: You will succeed if you act properly, maintain and develop inner calm.

    Nine in the third place: Beware of conflicts which may entangle you.

    Nine in the fourth place: This is a time when activity begins again and advancement is likely, radiating influence everywhere.

    Six in the fifth place: Your inner weakness hinders you from undertaking any new ventures, or from achieving recognition.

    Six at the top: Only complete acceptance can allay any deadlock, conflict, or even hatred, that will arise out of arrogance and stubbornness.
- **Fortune**: Fairly good.
- **Marriage**: Harmonious.
- **Children**: Stubborn.
- **Health**: Good.
- **Employment/Business**: Success.
- **Finance**: Good and stable.

35. CHIN–Progress

- The two trigrams are Li (Sun) and K'un (earth).
- These trigrams symbolise increasing influence, easy progress and prosperity.
- While the sun denotes activity, passion and progressiveness, the earth is passive, receptive and logical.
- There is warning here of possible separation, undue haste, and incorrect relationships.
- **The Judgement**: For the foundation of progress in great matters, the hexagram symbolises an independent but obedient servant, and a just and understanding master.
- **The Image**: The wise gain in virtue and self-reliance by shedding off the shabby and the unprincipled.
- **The Lines**

   Six at the bottom: Lacking confidence in others, your progress lies in persistence.

   Six in the second place: A time of difficulty followed by harmony.

   Six in the third place: A time of possible loss as also of advancement. Since everybody is in harmony, this common will and energy smoothens your path of all doubts about your own shortcomings.

   Nine in the fourth place: Conflict is likely, for your nature to store up treasures alienates you from others.

   Six in the fifth place: A time of progress, but remain reserved in an influential and creative position, for regret is foolish.

Nine at the top: This is the time for firm and punitive action to restore correct conditions.
- **Fortune**: Extremely good.
- **Marriage**: Ideal.
- **Children**: Intelligent, talented, obedient and loyal.
- **Health**: Good, but care of stomach is needed.
- **Employment/Business**: Prosperous.
- **Finance**: Good.

36. MING I–Darkening of the Light

- The trigram, K'un (earth) is above Li (sun or light).
- These two trigrams represent approaching nightfall, or light fading.
- This hexagram denotes accumulation of hostile or negative forces, with the omnipotence of an authority being against one's beliefs.
- Relationships may be sadly infirm, and none seems to be aware of your conditions which seem hateful to you.
- **The Judgement**: Constantly working at improving one's virtues should prepare you to take action when a favourable time comes.
- **The Image**: Be cautious, reserved and considerate, and avoid open enmity by immodest behaviour.
- **The Lines**
  Nine at the bottom: A time of mixed fortune. One attempts to avoid danger by ignoring it, and since some plans misfire, one withdraws.

Six in the second place: A time of promotion is indicated. The subject is inured and receives help, or he renders help to others in the same condition.

Nine in the third place: Expect real trouble to rebound, for this is a time of conflict.

Six in the fourth place: Others will help, but troubles are in store as danger lurks.

Six in the fifth place: Restrain yourself and remain active but accepting.

Six at the top: Though suffering is nearing its end, it is better to be cautious in holding on to what is established, and of difficulties after progress.

- **Fortune**: Extremely bad.
- **Marriage**: Not good.
- **Children**: Cause problems.
- **Health**: Average. Abdominal ailments likely.
- **Employment/Business**: Pretty bad.
- **Finance**: Heavy loss.

37. CHIA JEN–The Family

- This hexagram represents the family, its members, possessions and means of livelihood.
- Social institutions are also referred to in this hexagram.
- The importance of female dominance is highlighted by both trigrams.
- Indications are of a flourishing family.
- **The Judgement**: The woman in the family, being devoted, loyal and persevering, holds the family together in harmony.

- **The Image:** Sufficient energy, prevailing in the house is conserved by the man in the family behaving in a refined manner with speech control and gentle conduct.
- **The Lines**

    Nine at the bottom: A time of promotion, advance and recognition.

    Six on the second place: This is a time of improvement and success with stress on perseverance.

    Nine in the third place: The father needs to deal with matters with a firm hand, without being excessive. A tendency towards bad habits.

    Six in the fourth place: With the woman steering the household skilfully, this is a time of prosperity and recognition.

    Nine in the fifth place: The father will win respect and confidence of all through love and virtue.

    Nine at the top: A time of success, recognition and reward is indicated, and the father, recognising his responsibilities and influence, must live up to them.
- **Fortune:** Good.
- **Marriage:** Successful.
- **Children:** Obedient and loyal.
- **Health:** Fairly good. Beware of bowel problems.
- **Employment/Business:** Good.
- **Finance:** Fairly good, though there will be tendency to spend unnecessarily.

38. K'UEI–Neutrality and Disunity

- The two trigrams are Li (the flame) above, and Tui (the lake) below.
- The flame movement is upward, while that of water is downward denoting disunity.
- This hexagram denotes latent or actual conflict.
- It also indicates a lethargic condition, separation or mental agony.
- **The Judgement**: Though there are practical obstacles which appear weighty, there is also indication that opposing elements can together be creative.
- **The Image**: During times of isolation or conflict with things or people, one should become magnanimous towards others while preserving one's individuality.
- **The Lines**

   Nine at the bottom: Guard against thoughtless mistakes while enduring bad conditions, for a temporary setback will be followed by success and progress.

   Nine in the second place: Misunderstanding may call for a compromise by which success results.

   Six in the third place: Though complicated and dangerous obstacles arise, harmony and good fortune will soon ensure.

   Nine in the fourth place: Loneliness due to one's antipathy can be avoided with the help of an empathetic partner. A time of help, safety amidst danger and harmony after trouble.

Six in the fifth place: Joining forces with a kindred spirit would be fruitful if the relationship is sincere.

Nine at the top: Troubles will disappear by a correct attitude.

- **Fortune**: Bad.
- **Marriage**: Not so good.
- **Children**: Unhelpful to parents.
- **Health**: Internal organs can be seriously affected.
- **Employment/Business**: Poor.
- **Finance**: Need to save a lot for the future.

39. CHIEN–Obstruction

- The trigram, K'an (water), is above the trigram Ken (mountain) which denotes that a temporary lake in the mountain can suddenly result in its water crashing down on the villages and crops below.
- An abyss in front of a mountain indicates danger or difficulty of movement.
- This hexagram denotes a condition—a condition beset with obstacles that obstruct progress.
- The difficulties can be overcome by extreme caution.
- **The Judgement**: A harmonious attitude needs to be maintained; so one has to guard against being pressurised into adopting conventional or useless solutions.
- **The Image**: One has to develop sensitivity to one's condition and an attitude which creates harmony.
- **The Lines**

Six at the bottom: A time of neutral fortune, when nothing new should be undertaken.

Six in the second place: Though beset with difficulties, a definite commitment and acceptance will be fruitful.

Nine in the third place: Be cautious in your progress, and favourable unions or promotion will follow.

Six in the fourth place: It will be in your favour to be cautious, humble and diligent now, and wait for a favourable time.

Nine in the fifth place: Seemingly insurmountable problems can be faced with equanimity, and help and good fortune are sure to follow.

Six at the top: Seek the help of the wise and strong, and face problems with an unselfish attitude, for progress and recognition are sure to follow.

- **Fortune**: Bad.
- **Marriage**: Love affairs likely with others.
- **Children**: Will cause toil and pain for you.
- **Health**: Serious ailments likely.
- **Employment/Business**: Not profitable.
- **Finance**: Not healthy.

40. HSIEH–Liberation

- This hexagram indicates spring or early morning both of which signify new life and opportunities.
- The symptoms of imminent salvation or success signal the danger of relaxing prematurely.
- Any activity taken up now will be interrupted by past troubles.

- After hardship, fortunes will smile.
- **The Judgement**: New opportunities and conditions returning to normalcy should be tackled with care, and not overenthusiasm.
- **The Image**: Clear misunderstandings with forgiveness, for clarity in life is very fulfilling.
- **The Lines**

  Six at the bottom: Having endured past difficulties well, peace prevails and success is indicated.

  Nine in the second place: A man's natural skill will require less spontaneity and more consideration for promotion and success.

  Six in the third place: Despite apparently good times, one needs to be careful and correct.

  Nine in the fourth place: One must shed off the bad influence or else one will lose the better fortune which lies in the future.

  Six in the fourth place: This is a time of success with inner resolve, worthwhile actions and correct attitudes.

  Six at the top: Someone who has a bad attitude and has acquired unwarranted importance, must quickly relinquish them, so that promotion, recognition and success flow in.
- Fortune: Fairly good.
- **Marriage**: Very good.
- **Children**: Good.
- **Health**: Fairly good.
- **Employment/Business**: Promotion and profit.
- **Finance**: Improvement in status.

41. SUN–Decrease

- The trigram Ken (mountain) on top symbolises decrease, while the lower trigram, Tui (lake) suggests the mountain's edge crashing into the lake.
- But while the mountain suggests decrease by its crumbling, the lake denotes increase by receiving the crumbling edges.
- This hexagram symbolises one man's loss as another man's gain.
- Adjustment to this time is the focus of this hexagram.
- **The Judgement**: One can achieve a lot by understanding the inevitability of time, with austerity, simplicity and humility being right and proper.
- **The Image**: You may lose friends, or find things decreasing, but by readjusting your values, you can improve your character considerably.
- **The Lines**

Nine at the bottom: This is a time when you might help others and gain their approval.

Nine in the second place: Keep your integrity at all costs, for you will be prevailed upon to assist in something that goes against the grain.

Six in the third place: One of the three in an impossible triangle will go and find another relationship. A time of help from others.

Six in the fourth place: Bad times seem to vanish giving way to eager people helping without any obligation.

Six in the fifth place: A time of natural good luck.
Nine at the top: Success coming from unselfishness, recognition and respect are indicated.
- **Fortune**: Fairly good.
- **Marriage**: Ideal.
- **Children**: Good and well-mannered.
- **Health**: Needs attention.
- **Employment/Business**: Fairly good.
- **Finance**: Initial loss with gain later.

42. I–Increase

- The upper trigram Sun, and the lower trigram Chen, together present a picture of a luxuriant forest, full of blooming plants.
- The hexagram also suggests consideration and service by the strong.
- You will get assistance from somebody for your improvement.
- Good fortunes and benefits are on the increase.
- **The Judgement**: Since the time of increase is not permanent, now is the time to act without hesitation.
- **The Image**: Though there is good fortune and gain, there is need for caution, without hesitation.
- **The Lines**
  Nine at the bottom: Use this time for achievement and beware of selfishness. A time of tremendous success.
  Six in the second place: Success is assured due to one's inward love of god.

Six in the third place: Wise people, in harmony with the times, and having neutral authority, will be blessed with success and new responsibilites.

Six in the fourth place: A time of fresh responsibilities and successful opportunities.

Nine in the fifth place: A time of more responsibilities, self-improvement, promotion and successful opportunities.

Nine at the top: You need a concentrated, calm and reflective attitude, for this is a time of dislike, insults, retribution and loss.

- **Fortune**: Extremely good.
- **Marriage**: Harmonious.
- **Children**: Happy and fine.
- **Health**: Beware of stomach and throat ailments; likely to be affected by venereal disease.
- **Employment/Business**: Good.
- **Finance**: Unexpected windfall.

43. KUAI–Determination

- The two trigrams, above Ch'ien (heaven) and below Tui (lake), indicate a decision or breakthrough after a prolonged period of tension.
- This is a time when the inferior starts losing ground.
- There is a force which can create good or cause unpleasantness and disharmony everywhere.
- The focus of this hexagram is on this force or energy which needs to be channelled.

- **The Judgement**: With great determination and firmness, one needs to correct one's faults and be honest and open.
- **The Image**: The person, being strong and influential, shares his wealth, thus avoiding isolation.
- **The Lines**

  Nine at the bottom: A time of conflict caused by immodesty.

  Nine in the second place: Reason will triumph over passion when danger sets in. Quiet, working people may benefit.

  Nine in the third place: Good fortune follows by maintaining correct behaviour and attitudes, and also thus avoiding unpleasantness with others.

  Nine in the fourth place: Beware of being too obstinate, assertive or restless, and understand the nature of the obstacles ahead.

  Nine in the fifth place: Remain resolute and principled, for the time of difficulties will give way to achievement.

  Six at the top: Be vitally aware of the destructive forces which can undo achievements, and conflicts, bitterness and family complications can set in.
- **Fortune**: Fairly good.
- **Marriage**: Frustrations set in.
- **Children**: Arrogant and troublesome.
- **Health**: Special care needed.
- **Employment/Business**: Failure and losses.
- **Finance**: Fortune after poverty.

44. KOU–Tempting

- The trigram Ch'ien (heaven) is above Sun (wind, wood), and the strong force Ch'ien meets the feminine and penetrating force, Sun.
- This suggests that an authoritative and stable person is influenced by a weak but effective element.
- There is warning of unexpected encounters, accidents or misfortunes.
- Care should be taken in dealing with people seemingly good but with bad intentions.
- **The Judgement**: Profound insight and virtue are required to recognise people with ulterior motives who from inferior positions, rise to positions of power.
- **The Image**: Be humble and sensitive to the changing forces which surround you.
- **The Lines**

    Six at the bottom: Control must be exercised over an inferior element creeping in, or an unchecked desire.

    Nine in the second place: This being a time of assistance and promotion, one should keep all inferior or dangerous elements under control.

    Nine in the third place: Misfortune is indicated, and one can escape from danger by insight.

    Nine in the fourth place: Conflict and slander are in store.

    Nine in the fifth place: Be consistent and firm in your behaviour to receive benefit from 'soft' people. A time of help and recognition.

    Nine at the top: Be composed after withdrawing from the bad elements, for difficulties ahead are indicated.

- **Fortune**: Bad.
- **Marriage**: Not good.
- **Children**: Behaviour needs to be checked.
- **Health**: Great care needed.
- **Employment/Business**: Neither profitable.
- **Finance**: Low income.

45. TS'UI–In Accord

- The trigram Tui (lake) above Kun (earth) suggests water collection, symbolising people in accord.
- The warning is against disorder.
- A time for establishing conditions of stability and durability.
- This hexagram also promises promotion and success.
- The Judgement: Acting in accord, communities can achieve prosperity.
- The Image: Though there is harmony and accord, sudden danger can come from the group, or from outside.
- **The Lines**

Six at the bottom: The group should recognise its leader, its needs and its solution. A time of difficulty followed by good fortune.

Six in the second place: A time of help and promotion.

Six in the third place: Being isolated and humiliated, one must be cautious and resolute. Difficulties will be followed by relief.

Nine in the fourth place: One is respected for one's selfless service, but trouble is also indicated, brought about by one's incorrect conduct or disputes.

Nine in the fifth place: Deal directly, openly and be principled in dealing with people gathered around. Difficulties and disharmony are indicated.

Six at the top: A time of sadness, unsettled conditions, and lamentation.

- Fortune: Extremely good.
- Marriage: Happy.
- Children: Many, living in harmony.
- Health: Good. Beware of food poisoning.
- Employment/Business: Very good.
- Finance: Very good.

46. SHENG–Pushing Upward

- The time being spring, plants (trigram Sun –wood) push upward through the earth (trigram K'un), denoting growth and expansion.
- The focus is on growth rather than movement, or upward motion rather than simple expansion.
- In order to make the movement harmonious, one needs will power and control.
- This hexagram symbolises expansion and growth, and thereby, progress.
- **The Judgement**: Unselfish application, correct attitudes, and the advice of an authoritative person will now create harmony and lasting conditions.
- **The Image**: A wise person, being in harmony with fate, is sensitive and determined.
- **The Lines**

Six at the bottom: One's position is now insignificant, but one's efforts will bring success beyond expectation.

Nine in the second place: With limited resources, the subject progresses, and his inner soundness compensates for his outward lack of style. A time of advance and sadness.

Nine in the third place: The subject will choose the line of least resistance, achieving his goal, but his good fortune will not last.

Six in the fourth place: Travel is favoured, and one will reach one's goal, attaining special influence.

Six in the fifth place: Success can only come through correct and persistent effort, and care should be taken against being careless and taking shortcuts.

Six at the top: Only conscious, consistent effort can sustain the headlong progress.

- **Fortune**: Extremely good.
- **Marriage**: Very successful.
- **Children**: Well-mannered, loyal and obedient.
- **Health**: Good.
- **Employment/Business**: Very good.
- **Finance**: Smoothly flowing.

47. K'UN–Oppression

- The trigram K'an (water) lies below the trigram Tui (lake), suggesting exhaustion, or water being drained from the lake.
- The lines in the trigrams denote restriction, obstacles and oppression.
- This hexagram symbolises poverty, difficulty and oppression, and is one of the four dangerous hexagrams in I Ching.

- Your untiring efforts will not produce any gains.
- **The Judgement**: One has to learn from adverse conditions, and develop inner virtue unceasingly.
- **The Image**: One has to be aware of one's condition and limitations, and accepting them, be correct in one's attitudes and actions.
- **The Lines**

    Six at the bottom: One has to overcome delusions that difficulties are beyond one's capabilities to overcome them.

    Nine in the second place: Compromise, spiritual effort and patience are necessary to settle differences and find contentment.

    Six in the third place: In order to ward off shame, recognise the soft, peaceful way as the source of joy and inspiration.

    Nine in the fourth place: Do not compromise your humanitarian principles to please wealthy or powerful people.

    Nine in the fifth place: By maintaining one's composure, one can find relief.

    Six at the top: Resolute actions will pave the way for all problems to be wiped off completely.
- **Fortune**: Extremely bad.
- **Marriage**: Extremely unsuccessful.
- **Children**: No children, which causes heartache.
- **Health**: Serious and prolonged sickness.
- **Employment/Business**: Unfavourable.
- **Finance**: Low.

48. CHING–The Well

- The top trigram is K'an (water) into which is dipped a bucket represented by the trigram Sun (wood, plant).
- The plant (Sun) draws water upwards for sustenance, denoting depth and consistency.
- Depth symbolises man's sensitivity to the most profound needs of himself, whereas consistency implies dependability.
- The well is useful as a constant dependable source of water, just as a social structure must be depended on for justice and opportunity.
- **The Judgement**: Man's needs remain constant, just like the wells remain where they have always been. Beware of carelessness, neglect and insufficient depth.
- **The Image**: The image of good work, symbolised by the well, suggests that a useful well needs to be well-constructed, and for this, flexibility and unselfish appreciation of human nature are required.
- **The Lines**

  Six at the bottom: No appreciation of one's virtues leads to lack of incentive and thereby resulting in wastage of oneself.

  Nine in the second place: Cynicism and negligence could lead to tension and imminent troubles.

  Nine in the third place: Wait for conditions to improve and someone to recognise your potentials.

  Six in the fourth place: Put your plans into operation for inward progress.

Nine in the fifth place: One's spiritual, mental and material qualities will pave the way for success, profit and promotion.

Six at the top: One's openness and charity will benefit those around, and lead to one's own success.

- **Fortune**: Fairly good.
- **Marriage**: Good
- **Children**: Fine and happy.
- **Health**: Slow recovery from colds, urinary infection, and afflictions of lower part of the body.
- **Employment/Business**: Average.
- **Finance**: Insufficient funds.

49. KO–Revolution

- The trigram Tui (lake) above Li (fire) shows that two forces are in conflict.
- Tui and Li represent daughters, but here the younger has usurped her position, denoting revolution.
- The lines of the trigram suggest how to settle the conflicts that arise.
- This hexagram suggests that changes arise from conflicts, and conflicts arise from changes.
- **The Judgement**: This is not the right time to make changes, and one will be successful only if the changes are not for selfish motives.
- **The Image**: One, having the ability to understand changes taking place, notes the signs and is able to visualise the forthcoming problems and demands of the times, and be prepared for them.

- **The Lines**
  Nine at the bottom: Work hard, without being overambitious, try to avoid capitalising on current trends.
  Six in the second place: A time of good fortune and recognition.
  Nine in the third place: Excessive conservation or haste will be disastrous. So examine every situation thoroughly and discuss with those you trust.
  Nine in the fourth place: Be warned against pettiness and narrow-thinking. Promotion, good fortune and success for those with quiet lifestyles.
  Nine in the fifth place: Make decisive changes now, for fortune favours the bold.
  Six at the top: Only small changes are advisable. Be satisfied and obey rules of law.
- **Fortune**: Fairly good.
- **Marriage**: First marriage unfavourable. Second one favourable.
- **Children**: Need discipline.
- **Health**: Life in danger, with heart ailments.
- **Employment/Business**: Good.
- **Finance**: Good.

50. TING–The Cauldron

- The trigram Sun (wood) below Li (flame) fuels the flame, suggesting cooking in a cauldron, as the shape of the hexagram suggests.
- This hexagram represents nourishment and transformation.

- This hexagram, Ting, bodes well for established stable conditions, since the Chinese cauldron had three legs in ancient days, symbolising purity and stability.
- It symbolises the executive, judiciary and legislature, or father, mother and child, or husband, wife and mistress, etc.
- **The Judgement**: This hexagram focuses on practical values dedicated to higher principles.
- **The Image**: The wise man, realising that fate motivates the unique power in his life, lives life realistically, and by harmonising these forces, he enjoys good fortune and spiritual progress.
- **The Lines**

    Six at the bottom: The virtuous and talented succeed, and success will be followed by sadness.

    Nine in the second place: One is confident of securing prosperity in a worth while undertaking.

    Nine in the third place: Difficulties can be overcome by virtue. Obstacles and losses will be followed by happiness.

    Nine in the fourth place: Bad luck, due to one's own fault, with little success, leads to failure.

    Six in the fifth place: A time of success and progress, due to one's virtue.

    Nine at the top: It is a time of achievement and recognition.
- **Fortune**: Good.
- **Marriage**: Successful.
- **Children**: Talented and highly educated.
- **Health**: Diabetes is likely.
- **Employment/Business**: Very good and profitable.
- **Finance**: Unexpected windfall likely.

51. CHEN–The Arousing

- Both trigrams, being Chen, indicate a favourable time for a second chance.
- Chen, the arousing, is represented by a stimulating force or one which threatens and scatters.
- The emphasis is on restrained and skilful action and moderation in everything.
- Suppression gives way to arousal.
- **The Judgement**: One's composure will see one through catastrophic conditions with a harmonious and effective spirit.
- **The Image**: Disaster and collapse can ensue, but the wise will discover strengths and weaknesses within him, and arrange his affairs accordingly.
- **The Lines**

  Nine at the bottom: Sudden events denote a change in one's fortune for the better.

  Six in the second place: Be firm and resolute, for troubles and loss are inevitable now.

  Six in the third place: Beware of being paralysed by the shock of danger, and respond actively to events dictated by inner truth and wisdom.

  Nine in the fourth place: Beware of a befuddled mind which will not react to trouble.

  Six in the fifth place: Keep a clear head during repeated troubles, and organise your affairs with insight.

  Six at the top: Be cautious and withdrawn, for misfortune is unavoidable.

- **Fortune**: Fairly good.
- **Marriage**: Remarriage is good.
- **Children**: Will cause distress initially, but later will bring happiness.
- **Health**: Needs care, especially the nervous system.
- **Employment/Business**: Success after initial hiccups.
- **Finance**: Promising.

52. KEN–Keeping Still

- Both trigrams being Ken (mountain, or keeping still), they indicate a complete stop to movement.
- This hexagram denotes achievement of inner peace.
- It deals with ways in which inner peace can be achieved.
- This also implies meditation.
- **The Judgement**: One who, after a restless period, achieves inner calm, achieves a calm control over mind, and begins to understand the illusion behind social custom and one's nature.
- **The Image**: For meditation, concentration and stillness are required, just as in a dangerous situation when only swift response to an enemy's action breaks this stillness. This stillness is the most effective preparation for any demanding activity.
- **The Lines**
  Six at the bottom: If you are moving, and doubts arise, it is better to pause or change direction, and if you are still, remain so.
  Six in the second place: A time of worry for one cannot communicate to other one's folly.

Nine in the third place: Be calm and peaceful instead of being arrogant and repressive.
Six in the fourth place: Do not face the pace, for perfect harmony is still far off.
Six in the fifth place: Being a time of advance and harmony one should guard one's tongue against idle chatter.
Nine in the sixth place: A time of harmony, tranquillity and good fortune.

- **Fortune**: Fairly good.
- **Marriage**: Not at all good.
- **Children**: Independent and strong.
- **Health**: Needs a lot of care.
- **Employment/Business**: Average.
- **Finance**: Average.

53. CHIEN–Development

- The above trigram is Sun (eldest daughter) and below is Ken (youngest son), both growing together.
- Just as a tree (Sun) grows on the mountain (Ken), so is the progress gradual.
- Movement, or gradual progress, brings well-being and happiness.
- Even fortune and happiness come gradually.
- **The Judgement**: Correct and gradual development of a relationship is considered the main requisite for a successful union.
- **The Image**: Personality must develop through patient perseverance, and Chien is favourable for anything developing gradually.

- **The Lines**
  Six at the bottom: Through mistakes one will learn while setting out on a demanding journey.
  Six in the second place: One should share one's fortunes, or put them to unselfish use, for there lies rest and safety.
  Nine in the third place: In this time of disharmony and loss, one should persevere without using force or aggressive actions.
  Six in the fourth place: Humility will help to avert danger until it is time to move on.
  Nine in the fifth place: Overtaking everyone and scaling heights, one then suffers from bitterness, but harmony will return, helped by adjustment.
- **Fortune**: Good.
- **Marriage**: Good and happy.
- **Children**: Obedient and honest.
- **Health**: Ears, nose, stomach and bowels need attention.
- **Employment/Business**: Good.
- **Finance**: Good.

54. KUEI MEI–The Marrying Maiden

- The trigram Chen above denotes arousing or eldest son, while the trigram Li below denotes the youngest daughter or the joyous.
- Thus, a young girl, with joy in her, follows an older man who has the quality of arousing.
- The marrying maiden has to attend to her husband's most intimate needs.

- This hexagram indicates impermanence, and violation of social ethics and conventions.
- **The Judgement**: One is involved with others since one is useful which is due to an unspoken need of others.
- **The Image**: One has to understand that one's position is somewhat artificial, and so one must do the expected. One should be austere in conduct.
- **The Lines**

    Nine at the bottom: A time of achievement of one accepts one's inferior position.

    Nine in the second place: One will be secure, though there is no advance.

    Six in the third place: By accepting a position which is lowly or uncertain, one can hope to succeed, but wait for the right time.

    Nine in the fourth place: A time for changing one's course and to find the appropriate opportunity.

    Six in the fifth place: Fulfilment, success and good fortune follow.

    Six at the top: Being unable to fill the role demanded, one's success is not duly rewarded.

- **Fortune**: Bad.
- **Marriage**: Failure.
- **Children**: Deceptive and wicked.
- **Health**: Care needed.
- **Employment/Business**: Difficulties and loss.
- **Finance**: Very poor.

55. FENG–Greatness

- The trigram Chen (thunder, arousing) is above Li (flame, chinging) denotes brilliant success.
- Abundance and brilliance are symbolised by the hexagram, though they are short-lived.
- This denotes a time to enjoy what one possesses without expectations.
- Spiritual expansion is possible during this time of greatness and abundance.
- **The Judgement**: The unselfish and benevolent attitude will start waning, giving way to arrogance and temper.
- **The Image**: Abundance can be created by applying energy and insight, and the wise person will avoid complacency being temperate and judicious.
- **The Lines**

   Nine at the bottom: This is a time of others' aid bringing reward, and a fruitful association.

   Six in the second place: Loss or difficulty is followed by good fortune if one establishes a good relationship with others.

   Nine in the third place: A time of loss and difficulty.

   Nine in the fourth place: Conditions of disharmony and restlessness are indicated, though opportunities arise.

   Six in the fifth place: A time of help, promotion and recognition.

   Six at the top: A time of conflict and difficulty, worry, loss, or illusions.
- **Fortune**: Fairly good.
- **Marriage**: Not good.

- **Children**: Will be happy.
- **Health**: Guard against diabetes and abdominal disorders.
- **Employment/Business**: Very good and profitable.
- **Finance**: Sound and healthy.

56. LU–The Stranger

- Li (fire) is above Ken (mountain), symbolising a fire on the mountain, which is short-lived.
- While one moves, the other is still, and are strangers to each other.
- This hexagram Lu indicates a person who is one of life's travellers.
- A real, inner motive prompts travels.
- **The Judgement**: The traveller must be flexible, sincere and adjusting and reserved in his manner for he is vulnerable to demanding or grasping people.
- **The Image**: Being temporary, the mountain fire symbolises a person who does not get involved with attitudes or events that will complicate his life.
- **The Lines**

    Six at the bottom: Be cautious while in a vulnerable position, and respect others' attitudes.

    Six in the second place: A time of progress and success, possibly through travel.

    Nine in the third place: There is trouble within one's own environment, and others are unsympathetic towards the traveller.

Nine in the fourth place: Though a time of success and travel, one will feel restricted success and travel, one will feel restricted and uncomfortable with the situation.

Six in the fifth place: A time of success, reward and promotion.

Nine at the top: One loses one's flexibility and modesty due to one's reckless, arrogant and cynical behaviour.

- Fortune: Fairly bad.
- Marriage: Not good.
- Children: Lonely, unlucky and not in harmony with parents.
- Health: Danger to the respiratory and digestive systems.
- Employment/Business: Very bad.
- Finance: Depleting.

57. SUN–The Penetrating Wind

- Both trigrams being Sun, they symbolise the wind, the gentle or penetrating quality.
- They also denote harmony.
- Sun also symbolises plants which bend with the wind, denoting flexibility and harmony.
- Auguring well for new undertakings, Sun also helps in developing a non-wilful attitude towards people.
- **The Judgement**: This is a time of influencing more strength of character than by direct action.
- **The Image**: The wise person paves the way for what is to follow, following suggestions and leadership.

- **The Lines**
  Six at the bottom: Conditions are uncertain, and one must advance if the path is clear, else withdraw.
  Nine in the second place: Be open and honest in order to succeed. A good fortune for communication and academics.
  Nine in the third place: A time of sudden advance or difficulty.
  Six in the fourth place: A time of success and good luck, when a person in a responsible position makes full use of his resources.
  Nine in the fifth place: One needs to have a careful reform, and be prepared to continue changes till the right time.
  Nine at the top: Success may be short-lived, and loss and difficulties are likely.
- Fortune: Not good.
- Marriage: Not good.
- Children: Obedient, but need discipline.
- Health: Guard against diabetes and venereal diseases.
- Employment/Business: Fairly profitable.
- Finance: You will spend all you earn.

58. TUI – Joyousness

- Both trigrams are Tui, denoting the joyous, the youngest daughter or lake.
- The youngest daughter, while singing, radiates cheerfulness and joy.
- Tui also symbolises success and prosperity.

- In relationship you will have the opportunity to communicate more deeply than before.
- **The Judgement:** Joy here is uncomplicated and infectious, and along with perseverance, forms an ideal balance of qualities.
- **The Image:** The two lakes joining symbolise happiness, knowledge and wisdom.
- **The Lines**

  Nine at the bottom: A time of harmony, secure, self contained contentment, and freedom from desire and compulsion, but beware of becoming complacent or selfish.

  Nine in the second place: A time of harmony and progress, but be warned of getting involved in low pleasures.

  Six in the third place: A time of being deceived into making dangerous mistakes, and tempted into worthless, unfulfilling pleasures.

  Nine in the fourth place: Caution will lead one to material advance and pleasure, without compulsion or greed.

  Nine in the fifth place: One has to avoid danger by avoiding becoming involved with unworthy people.

  Six at the top: A time of helpful or pleasant circumstances with little success, when one is swept along by fate.
- Fortune: Fairly good.
- Marriage: Remarriage good.
- Children: Harmonious with parents.
- Health: Fairly good.
- Employment/Business: Good and prosperous.
- Finance: Trickles in.

59. HUAN–Dispersion

- The trigram Sun (wind) is above K'an (water) indicating gusts of wind blowing the spume from the waves, that is, dispersion.
- Indications are of energies being dissolved leading to waste.
- There are also indications of how energy that is blocked up or stored can be released.
- This heralds the beginning of development and expansion.
- **The Judgement**: A person of great authority unites men divided by egoism, by sharing common, higher activities like religious ritual.
- **The Image**: The image is of a giver of charity, uniting others in common piety.
- **The Lines**

  Six at the bottom: A time of advance when vigorous and selfless action will prevent quarrelling and misunderstanding.

  Nine in the second place: A time of mixed fortune when one takes steps to establish firm, stable conditions within himself or externally.

  Six in the third place: It will be useful to renounce the self when one has to deal with stressful circumstances.

  Six in the fourth place: A time of mixed fortune and promotion when one needs to make all things cohesive.

  Nine in the fifth place: A time of good fortune and promotion when one needs to make all things cohesive.

  Nine at the top: A time of change for the better.

- Fortune: Fairly good.
- Marriage: Initial troubles, later happiness.
- Children: Troubled by them.
- Health: Guard against respiratory afflictions.
- Employment/Business: Good.
- Finance: Good.

60. CHIEH–Limitation

- The trigram K'an (water, danger) is above Tui (lake, the joyous), suggesting water overflowing from the lake unless restrained.
- Awareness of limitation and restrain in one's behaviour are required for achieving ideals and perfection.
- Limitations are indicated for those who can neither progress nor slide backwards.
- One should keep a good sense of balance, and avoid the extremes.
- **The Judgement**: One should keep a sense of proportion, and increase one's resources by exercising restraint, limitations and thrift.
- **The Image**: One can follow a particular path by avoiding being pulled in any direction, and determining one's talents and weakneses, bearing in mind the limitations ahead.

The Lines

Nine at the bottom: It is wise to be discreet and patient for the right time to make advances.

Nine in the second place: When the time for action comes, make the most of it.

Six in the third place: Beware of any extravagance which will have harsh repercussions.

Six in the fourth place: A time for rewards by right conduct.

Nine in the fifth place: Great achievements are possible if one can impose limits on others which the situation warrants, and which do not restrain their freedom.

Six at the top: Misfortune will accrue if one persists in one's attitudes or actions that people resent.

- Fortune: Fairly good.
- Marriage: Good.
- Children: Obedient and loyal.
- Children: Needs care of nervous disorders and abdominal problems.
- Employment/Business: Wait for better times.
- Finance: Not sound.

61. CHUNG FU–Understanding

- Sun (eldest daughter, the gentle) is above Tui (youngest daughter, the joyous), suggesting the older sister's gentle influence on the younger one to follow happily.
- This hexagram symbolises confidence and sincerity.
- The weak or the inferior is stimulated gently by the powerful.
- The weaker element responds with joy and confidence.
- **The Judgement**: Influence is possible even over the most stubborn through the power of universal truth or understanding, or awareness of the divine spirit.

- **The Image**: Penetrating understanding is a requisite for transcending social, cultural or other differences between people.
- **The Lines**
  Nine at the bottom: A time of success, hard work and help from others, and warning against deviousness or selfish judgement.
  Nine in the second place: A time of good fortune for the virtuous.
  Six in the third place: Gain and loss fluctuate.
  Six in the fourth place: Promotion as well as separation are likely.
  Nine in the fifth place: A time of harmony and achievement through indiscriminating empathy with all.
  Nine at the top: A time of difficulty or complication, and it is wise to be modest and humble.
- Fortune: Good.
- Marriage: Ideal.
- Children: Harmonious and sincere.
- Health: Fairly good.
- Employment/Business: Good.
- Finance: Steady increase.

62. HSIAO KUA–Excess of the Small

- The trigram Ken (the mountain) is below Chen (thunder, arousing), denoting strength trapped by the force above.
- One is unable to meet the demands of the situation, suggested by the powerful being contained by the weak.

- Lack of steady progress, or meanness, is indicated here.
- A small excess or mistake prevents achievement.
- The Judgement: By recognising one's limitations and by being conscientious, one's virtue help overcome difficulties.
- The Image: One must pay strict attention to the form, the custom, and behaviour.
- **The Lines**

  Six at the bottom: A time of good fortune followed by loss.

  Six in the second place: Be conscientious when you find yourself in a situation for which you are unprepared.

  Nine in the third place: Great caution is vital against being overconfident, careless or vulnerable.

  Nine in the fourth place: A time of temporary difficulty, but a cautious and conciliatory approach is necessary.

  Six in the fifth place: A person will succeed through his real achievements and good qualities.

  Six at the top: Only hardworking, modest people can hope for good fortune now.
- Fortune: Bad.
- Marriage: Separation likely.
- Children: Disharmony with parents, and among themselves.
- Health: Extreme care needed. Diabetes and chest ailments likely.
- Employment/Business: Extremely bad.
- Finance: Moderate.

63. CHI CHI–Completion

- The trigram K'an (water) above Li (fire) denotes completion through boiling water.
- This is a time of success, harmony and fruition.
- This also denotes that these successes will be short-lived.
- This hexagram suggests a harmonious union.
- The Judgement: The successful period brought about by a peak of energies should be used for undertaking only small matters now, and accept the fact that decay must follow fruition.
- The Image: What is incomplete should be brought to fruition without delay.
- **The Lines**

    Nine at the bottom: A time of difficulty when one should not undertake anything.

    Six in the second place: A time of difficulty or loss.

    Nine in the third place: A time of difficulty and conflict will be followed by success with perseverance.

    Six in the fourth place: A time of caution against lurking dangers.

    Nine in the fifth place: Be modest and simple, and avoid outward shows of virtue.

    Six at the top: A time of opportunity, and bad influence can be concealed by stable circumstances.
- Fortune: Fairly good.

- Marriage: Very good.
- Children: Blessed and happy.
- Health: Good.
- Employment/Business: Fairly good.
- Finance: Trickling in.

64. WEI CHI–Before Completion

- The trigram Li (flame) is above K'an (water), denoting the sun arising from the sea at dawn.
- The time being spring, a time of effort and preparation for completion is essential.
- This hexagram holds great hope for the future.
- This suggests that there will be changes for the better.
- The Judgement: Conscious, contemplative attitudes will ensure security in a hostile situation.
- The Image: One should examine the nature of one's circumstances, for fire moving upwards and water flowing downwards show an irreconcilable situation.
- **The Lines**

    Six at the bottom: Refrain from advancing till the way is clear for achievement for success will be unrewarding.

    Nine in the second place: A time when unusual or unplanned manoeuvres to advance is disastrous.

    Six in the third place: Withdraw, make a break, and start a new activity.

Nine in the fourth place: A time of success and profit, possibly a dangerous situation also, but grab the opportunity while the going is good.

Six in the fifth place: A time of success, and be empathic and orderly.

Nine at the top: Be warned against excess or carelessness, for one has already achieved harmony.

- Fortune: Fairly good.
- Marriage: Good.
- Children: Good.
- Health: Beware of heart and abdominal afflictions.
- Employment/Business: Successful.
- Finance: Needs a watch.